Mastering Math through Magic
Grades 2-3

* * * * * * * * * *

Mary A. Lombardo

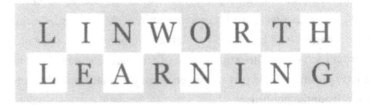

A Publication of Linworth Learning

Linworth Publishing, Inc.
Worthington, Ohio

Library of Congress Cataloging-in-Publication Data

Lombardo, Mary A.
    Mastering math through magic, grades 2-3 / by Mary A. Lombardo.
        p. cm.
    Includes bibliographical references and index.
    ISBN 1-58683-133-X
    1. Magic tricks in mathematics education. 2. Mathematics—Study and teaching
(Elementary) I. Title.

QA20.M33L663 2003
372.7—dc21

2003043321

Published by Linworth Publishing, Inc.
480 East Wilson Bridge Road, Suite L
Worthington, Ohio 43085

ISBN: 1-58683-133-X

5 4 3 2 1

Table of Contents

✳ ✳ ✳ ✳ ✳ ✳ ✳ ✳ ✳ ✳ ✳

About the Author

✳ ✳ ✳ ✳ ✳ ✳ ✳ ✳ ✳ ✳ ✳

 Mary Lombardo is a retired teacher who has taught all grades from one through six and has taught reading to at-risk students. For several years she worked in an alternative public school program for homeschooled students, providing curriculum and teaching assistance to parents and half-day instruction to students. She also served as a teacher trainer for the Albuquerque Public Schools.

Mary is proof that life after retirement is busier than ever. She writes, works as a volunteer mediator, presents plays to seniors with a reader's theater group, records seniors' histories for their families, volunteers in church and civic groups, and travels with her husband, Nick, whenever they can. Mary has three adult children, who all live in the Southwest.

Math Skills Cross Reference Chart

Math Trick #	Match Trick Title	Page #	Addition	Doubling	Halving	Subtraction
1	Magic Nines	17	X			
2	Halfies	19	X	X	X	X
3	Number Split	21	X	X	X	X
4	Line 'Em Up	23				
5	Changeover	25	X	X	X	X
6	Flip 'Em	27	X			X
7	Flip 'Em Backward	29	X			X
8	Clock Opposites	31	X	X		X
9	Magic Toothpicks	33				
10	Family Numbers	35	X	X	X	X
11	Triple Trouble	37	X			X
12	How Old Are You?	39	X			X
13	Tricky Two-Step	41	X			X
14	Words and Numbers	43				
15	What's the Date?	47	X	X	X	X
16	Calendar Opposites	49	X	X		
17	When Were You Born?	52	X	X		X
18	The Very Day	54	X	X		X
19	Transparent Dice	58	X			X
20	Crazy Eight	60	X	X		X
21	Roll 'Em Partner	62	X	X	X	X
22	I've Got Your Number	64	X	X	X	X
23	Evening the Odds	69	X			
24	Leftovers, Anyone?	71				X
25	Hidden Coins	74	X			X
26	Whatever You Say	76	X			
27	Penny Pick	78	X		X	X
28	Funny Feet	82				
29	Lucky Lengths	84	X			X
30	Double Magic	86	X	X		X

How to Use this Book

The Math Skills Cross Reference Chart

The Math Skills Cross Reference Chart on page iv gives the reader an at-a-glance look at which magic tricks apply to each of the math skills listed. The name of the math trick, as well as the page on which it is found, is listed, and an X indicates that the math skill is represented by the trick.

Be a magician yourself!

Before telling your students they are going to learn how to do magic tricks, perform some of the tricks in Chapters I through V and impress your class with your magical powers.

The tricks are easy to do; most of the props are already in use in your classroom or home; and easy-to-follow, step-by-step directions for the tricks are given.

Present the student introduction.

Use the teacher script as a student introduction to stimulate class interest in learning to do the magic tricks.

Review the basic math operations that are listed here.

Many of the magic tricks are based on the fundamental operations that follow. This would be a good time to practice these operations, as being familiar with them will make the reasoning behind the tricks easier to understand.

1. Doubling and halving numbers are a good introduction to multiplication and division.

    To double a number, you add it to itself or multiply it by 2.

$$6 + 6 = 12$$
$$6 \times 2 = 12$$

To halve a number you count how many 2's are in the number or divide it by 2.

$$2, 4, 6, 8, 10, 12 = six\ 2's\ in\ all$$
$$12\ divided\ by\ 2 = 6$$

A simple way to teach students how to halve a number is to have them count by 2's until they reach the designated number, jotting down a line or check for every number they say. This is especially helpful when they are dealing with a large number.

Example: When counting up to 20 they will end up with 10 lines or 10 2's.

2 4 6 8 10 12 14 16 18 20
/ / / / / / / / / /

Counting in this way will lead to using vocabulary ("There are 10 2's in 20." "Half of 20 is 10.") that helps in beginning to understand multiplication and division. Another way to determine how many 2's are in a number is to draw a corresponding number of lines and draw circles around pairs. Calculators can also be used.

2. Doubling a number and then splitting it in half brings back the original number. Many of the tricks use this relationship as well as the opposite functions of addition and subtraction to work their magic.

3. If you have three evenly spaced numbers, subtracting the amount between the numbers from the third number and adding the amount between the numbers to the first number gives you two numbers equal to the center one.

7, 11, 15 are spaced 4 numbers apart
15 − 4 = 11 and 7 + 4 = 11

Once you've reviewed and practiced the operations shown above, it's time to get into the magic!

Start with the easiest tricks.

The easiest tricks in the book are marked in the introduction to each chapter with a double asterisk(**). They serve as a good introduction to the magic unit. As you perform the tricks, ask the students how they think the magic works. Test their ideas to see if they are correct.

Go over the directions step by step, either reading them to the students or copying the directions for use on an overhead projector and reading them together. The students should practice the trick in pairs or small groups and, if no correct theories have been advanced, again ask if anyone can guess what makes the trick work.

After reading the explanation of how the trick works found under the heading **"Why does this work?"** ask the students to explain in their own words how the magic works and, if appropriate, write an equation to express the math behind the magic.

Copy and distribute the student handout. Complete the **"How did you do?"** section together, with students writing the answers in their own words.

Continue in this manner with the remainder of the tricks in the first five chapters.

Teacher Introduction

* * * * * * * * * * *

The successful completion of most magic tricks depends a great deal on diversion. A skilled magician will divert the audience's attention so tricks can be performed without anyone seeing or deducing exactly what is happening. Each trick in this book uses some form of diversion so that, even though the tricks are simple, the audience cannot guess how the magic is performed.

Mastering Math through Magic uses diversion, too. As students focus on learning magic tricks, they don't realize that they are improving their knowledge of how numbers work and are practicing basic math skills. Learning by doing something enjoyable is an effective way to learn and retain information and skills. This book provides a fun way to review and practice math skills for everyday use, as well as for the math and reading testing that is federally mandated in grades three through eight.

You can use this book in several ways:

- Use the tricks to practice math skills in the classroom with every student checking to see that the math done by the magician and the volunteer is correct. Here would be a good place to incorporate practice using calculators.
- Present a simple or an extravagant magic show.
- Plan an entire integrated unit around the magic tricks.
- Give individual students the directions for a trick and the time to perform it in class as a fun reward for some job well done.

The National Council of Teachers of Mathematics (NCTM) suggests that to keep students interested in math, present them with activities that will interest and challenge them as well as help them develop a sense of numbers. Whichever way you decide to use the information in this book, you will be following that suggestion.

Organization of the Book

After this introductory section for the teacher, there is a short teacher script to help introduce the magic unit to the students.

Five chapters of tricks follow. Each chapter begins with a listing of the tricks that follow, outlining the math skills covered so they can be assigned to ensure that all students find both challenge and success.

Chapter I includes tricks that are very simple. If you are presenting a magic show, these tricks should be done one time only, as the answer is always the same. The tricks in **Chapter II** use calendars while those in **Chapter III** involve the use of dice. Coins are the basis of the magic in **Chapter IV.** The tricks in **Chapter V** use rulers and tape measures.

Then the magic begins! The tricks are written in easy-to-follow, step-by-step directions to facilitate instruction.

Each trick begins with a short introductory statement for the students to use to announce what they plan to do. The tricks themselves are organized in a three-part format.

1. **THE PROPS** part tells what **materials** are needed to do the trick.
2. **THE TRICK** gives step-by-step directions for performing the trick with suggestions for what the students should say.
3. **THE MAGIC** explains how the trick works mathematically.

Examples and illustrations are included to help the teacher explain how the tricks work and to make performing and understanding the tricks easier.

At the end of each trick, there is a student handout with some questions under the heading **"How did you do?"** which the students should answer in their own words. This exercise gives them the opportunity to review what they have done and to write the math equations they used to demonstrate that they understand the math reasoning behind the trick.

Objectives

This book was written with the following objectives in mind:

1. Correlate teaching and learning activities with the concepts contained in the math standards as set forth by the National Council of Teachers of Mathematics.

The National Council of Teachers of Mathematics (NCTM) has developed a set of 10 standards for math learning from pre-kindergarten through grade 12. The tricks in *Mastering Math through Magic* correlate with the concepts presented in these standards.

2. Teach children that working with numbers can be fun.

When students look forward to presenting magic tricks, they approach the task with pleasure, not fear, and build confidence in their abilities to work with numbers.

3. Cultivate a sense of numbers.

Number sense is a familiarity with how numbers work. Students with number sense can predict what will happen in number situations and have increased flexibility when working with numbers.

4. Increase fluency in mental manipulation of numbers.

As students become more familiar with the logical way that numbers work, they will be able to do many math functions mentally.

5. Understand the relationships between number operations.

Many of the tricks depend on reversing operations to make the "magic" work. Students see that addition and subtraction, and doubling and halving, are opposites.

6. Provide an opportunity for students to write about what they have done and learned.

Research shows that writing about math operations cements understanding. After each trick, students write about their performances and review the mathematical reasons and equations that make the trick work.

7. Improve confidence in one's knowledge of numbers by successfully participating in performance of magic tricks.

Subject matter is best learned and remembered through play. Because students are focused on mastering a magic trick, they are more relaxed about learning. Complexity of the tricks varies so all children are challenged and can participate successfully.

8. Serve as an introduction to multiplication and division.

Learning how to double and halve numbers leads to an understanding of multiplication and division.

Correlation with National Math Standards

The tricks, games, and the suggested processes for creating mathematical games and designing magic tricks in *Mastering Math through Magic* correspond to the concepts presented in the math standards issued by the NCTM for students from pre-kindergarten through grade 12. In the listings that follow, the corresponding math concepts are shown in bold print.

For a complete description of the math standards, refer to the NCTM Web site at <www.nctm.org>.

Correlation of Magic Tricks to Math Concepts

In the following listing, all of the tricks in this book correlate with every concept with the exception of *Magic Toothpicks* and *The Magic Number*. These two tricks are based on trickery, not math functions. They are included to provide a bit of humor!

NUMBER AND OPERATIONS

The math that underlies the magic in each trick demonstrates how numbers and number relationships work. Because each trick involves performing math operations, the tricks also encourage facility and accuracy in computing.

PROBLEM SOLVING

After each trick is performed and before the math explanation is read, students are asked to formulate a mathematical theory of why the magic works. As they theorize about the math operations used in the tricks, they use problem-solving techniques and build and review mathematical knowledge.

REASONING AND PROOF

The students conjecture about how the tricks work mathematically and evaluate their guesses to determine if they can prove they are correct.

COMMUNICATION

After each trick, the students complete a handout explaining in their own words the math that makes the magic work. Their communication must be clear, and they must demonstrate that they understand the math reasoning.

CONNECTIONS

All of the tricks use interconnecting mathematical ideas and operations. The connections between subtraction and addition, and doubling and halving, are clearly shown.

REPRESENTATION
The math operations in all of the tricks can be represented pictorially or by using objects.

MEASUREMENT
The tricks in **Chapter V, Measurement Malarkey**, call for use of rulers and tape measures.

Correlation of Games to Math Concepts
As students use their creativity and math knowledge to play mathematically related games, they

1. demonstrate that they understand number operations (**NUMBER AND OPERATIONS**);

2. use a variety of strategies to win games (**PROBLEM SOLVING**);

3. show or prove why their mathematical conjectures work (**REASONING AND PROOF**);

4. communicate their math ideas through explaining how a game is played (**COMMUNICATION**); and

5. use connections between number ideas and operations to form a winning strategy (**CONNECTIONS**).

If You Decide to Present a Magic Show

✷ ✷ ✷ ✷ ✷ ✷ ✷ ✷ ✷ ✷ ✷

Putting on a magic show does not have to be a big production. You have many options:

OPTION 1. The easiest way to have a magic show is to assign one trick to each student and present the tricks within your own classroom. Choose days when performances will be held and post a sign-up sheet so students can select when they want to perform. The advantages for doing it this way are:
- children have a chance to perform in front of an audience without using much class time;
- all students practice math skills as they check to see that the magician and the volunteer are doing the math operations correctly; and
- the magicians can explain the math process to their classmates, providing another opportunity to review skills and thought processes.

OPTION 2. Another fairly easy way to put on a show is to divide your class into several groups with each group responsible for a different chapter in the book. These groups can present their tricks to various classes in the school with each child responsible for assembling and carrying his or her own props.

One of the magicians also can act as emcee to start off the show. That child introduces the show and the first performer. Each child in turn, after performing his or her own magic trick, introduces the next person who will perform. The last person to perform is the emcee who closes the show, thanking the audience for its attention.

OPTION 3. The most time-consuming way to have a show is for each student in your class to learn one or more tricks and as a whole perform for other individual classes or at a school assembly. While this does take more planning and time, presenting a show of this nature will be one of your students' favorite memories of school.

If your class has organized and presented a show at your school, you might want to share the magic with others. Senior citizen centers or retirement homes are good venues for this type of show as are libraries that often offer presentations for school field trips.

Whichever option you choose, you won't have to worry that the assignment is a waste of study time. Learning how to perform the tricks can be done during the school day or can be assigned for homework or a combination of both. The tricks that your students will learn and practice fulfill every requirement for valuable study by furthering their understanding of how numbers work and by raising their comfort levels for math. In addition, motivation will be high and attitude will be positive, two of the most important factors for effective learning.

The Props

Most of the tricks call only for paper and marker. Using a large piece of paper posted where the audience can see it and using a dark colored marker are good ideas for two reasons. One, the audience can check to make sure the volunteer is following the directions and doing the math right—two points vital to the successful completion of the trick. Two, the audience will be able to see right away that the young magicians have done exactly what they said they would do.

Other simple props are pages from a calendar, preferably a large wall calendar so that the pages can be posted for the audience to see; a clock or picture of a clock face; coins, stones, or dried beans; regular dice; and toothpicks.

With tricks that use small objects such as coins or beans, use an overhead projector so the audience can see what is going on in the trick. If this is not possible, make sure the magician keeps the audience informed about what is happening.

In **Chapter II, Calendar Capers,** you will need to cut out a box that can be laid over a calendar page to show three rows of three on the calendar. This is the only prop that has to be made. All others are easily found at home or in the classroom.

The Dress

No matter what kind of show you plan, your young magicians will be concerned about what to wear.

Ask the children to recall magicians they have seen perform on television or in person and to describe what they wore. You might even take them to the library to find books about magicians to see the many different kinds of magician apparel. Some magicians are casual, wearing everyday clothes. Some magicians wear robes and turbans, some wear tails and top hats, and others wear nice suits or dresses.

The important thing to stress to your students is that whatever they choose to wear must be comfortable. If they have to worry about how their clothes are fitting or if the clothes have to be constantly adjusted, they won't be able to concentrate on performing the tricks.

To keep the costuming simple, students can wear their everyday school clothes or dress clothes. Pairing black pants and a black shirt makes another good magician outfit.

Making Costumes

If your students want to wear costumes, here are some ideas for making a star-studded cape, a bow tie, a top hat, and a turban. You will need the following materials:

- black oak-tag
- black construction and crepe papers
- black ribbon or string
- aluminum foil
- star stickers

e a cape:

enough black crepe paper to cover the back of the student
shoulder to shoulder.

ce of string or ribbon along the top edge, fold
ches, and either tape or staple a hem, making
ribbon in the staples so it can be used to

r stickers and larger star and
num foil. Attach the
nasking tape rolled

from each side so the
houlders, and tie the ribbon in front.

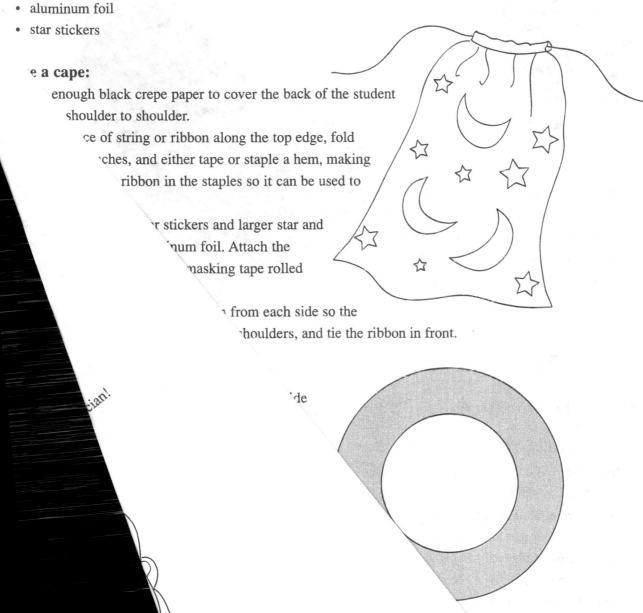

cian!   de

Linworth Learning

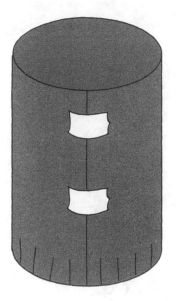

2. Take a large piece of construction paper and tape it into a cylinder so that it fits in the circle you have cut. This is the top of the hat. Cut it down a few inches if it is too tall. Cut one-inch wide slits all around one end.

3. When you fold up the cut pieces and glue them onto the bottom of the brim, the top hat is ready to wear. Additional stars and sky shapes can be pasted to the underside of the brim.

4. Complete the hat by fashioning a bow tie from crepe paper of any color. Voila! Instant magi

To make a turban:

A turban instead of a top hat makes the costume more exotic, and that might appeal to some of your students.

1. Take a piece of cloth, a scarf, or a piece of crepe paper about four feet long and a foot wide. Drape it over the front of the head. Bring up the ends and crisscross them around the back of the head, then around the front as far as they will go. Tuck the ends under. A star sticker or aluminum foil cutout can be taped to the front of the turban.

Patter

A magic show is not just about doing magic tricks. The audience must be warmed up and put in a receptive frame of mind. One of the best ways to do this is for the performers to tell jokes or relate amusing incidents that have happened to them.

You can use one of your library periods to find joke books suitable for your young magicians to use, or you can assign this task as homework. Ask the students to choose several jokes, memorize them, and practice telling them.

Another homework assignment is for students to write one or more essays telling about something funny that has happened to them. If they intend to use some of these stories in their performances, they should practice telling them aloud.

The students also will have to create their own magic words to use as they perform their tricks. This would be a good time for a lesson in alliteration and rhyming. See The Language of Magic section in "Teacher Script for Student Introduction" for suggestions.

When they are learning the tricks, the students also should practice how they will give the directions for doing the tricks. Each trick includes suggested statements that the students can read, or they can make up their own patter as they work through the tricks.

Practice is very important. You cannot emphasize this point enough. The students should practice the jokes. They should practice what they will say throughout their tricks. They should practice performing the tricks. If they will be wearing costumes, they should have at least one practice session wearing them.

Using *Mastering Math through Magic* can be a valuable part of your math instruction. There is no better way to make students comfortable with working with numbers than to have them practice math skills in an enjoyable format, such as preparing for a magic show. You can enjoy the fun of a magic performance knowing that your students are learning.

Teacher Script for Student Introduction

You are going to become magicians. You will learn some mind-boggling magic tricks that will amaze your friends. Your friends will be asking, "How did you do that?" Of course, you won't tell because the secret to being a good magician is never revealing how the tricks work.

The tricks that you're going to learn will be easy for you to do, but it will be hard for your friends to figure out how you work your magic. You will be able to add numbers that you can't see, guess a secret number that someone has chosen, tell which numbers are rolled on dice without looking at the dice, and perform many more mystical tricks.

Some of the tricks you will do are simple and some are more challenging, but I promise you, they are all puzzling and astonishing!

Getting Started

If you've watched some of the great magicians perform, you know that they don't just stand up and perform magic tricks. They usually tell the audience what to expect before they do the tricks and might tell a few jokes or stories to get everyone laughing and in a good mood.

Successful magicians rehearse and rehearse before they perform. They don't just practice their tricks. They also practice what they will say to the audience. You will want to do the same thing. You can find some good joke books at the library. Choose some jokes you like and memorize them. Practice telling the jokes and talking about what you will do in the trick. Do the tricks several times before you perform them for an audience, and your show will go smoother than a speedy slide across slippery ice.

Another thing to remember is not to reveal the answer to the trick too soon. Scratch your head, rub your chin and frown, as if you are thinking very hard before saying some magic words and revealing the answer. Acting this way will make the tricks seem more mystifying to your audience.

The Language of Magic

How do you learn the magic words to say? You make them up! Honest!

Magicians often use words that sound magical just before they demonstrate their magic powers. "Abracadabra, hocus pocus" are some famous magic words that you've probably heard many times. Just like famous magicians, you can make up and use any magic words you like. Try some rhymes like:

"Beetle juice and bat's wings,
I am the master of magical things."

Or just string some words together that start with the same letter and sound good like:

"Suffering saliva and salamander soup."

What Do Magicians Wear?

Now, what about clothes? What should you wear when you perform? Some magicians wear capes and top hats. Some dress in everyday clothes.

You can dress in a special outfit, something that you usually don't wear to school. Or you can borrow or make clothes that you think are just the thing for a magician to wear. If you decide you want to make a special outfit, I can help you with some ideas.

Whatever outfit you decide on, make sure you are comfortable in it, and don't worry about looking like a magician. Your tricks will show you are a real magician no matter what you are wearing.

Learning the Magic Tricks

I have a book that gives clear directions for doing many magic tricks. Each trick begins with one sentence that you can use to announce what you will be doing in the trick.

The directions for the tricks include some suggestions for what to say to your audience before and during the trick. Many of the directions for doing the tricks are short and easy, so you will be able to memorize the steps. Some of the tricks have more involved directions, so you might want to copy the steps onto small index cards that you can read from as you perform the trick.

We will need some props or materials to do each trick. Everything we need is either somewhere in our classroom or your house, or they are things that you can make or get easily.

For each trick in the book, there is a section called THE MAGIC. This explains, *for our eyes only,* how the trick works and gives you a place to write about how you performed the trick.

Now, on to the magic!

Chapter I
ONE-TIMERS

✳ ✳ ✳ ✳ ✳ ✳ ✳ ✳ ✳ ✳

Teacher Notes

There are 14 tricks in this chapter. Most use single step math processes with only a few calling for borrowing and carrying. All are easy to perform and easy to understand. The easiest are marked with a double asterisk (**).

      The answers to these tricks are always the same so, if used in performances, they should be done only one time. In tricks calling for a large piece of paper, make sure to place the paper where the audience can see what is being written.

Trick 1. Magic Nines: Addition**
In this trick, the magician will correctly predict which pile of cards a volunteer will choose.

Trick 2. Halfies: Addition, Subtraction, Halving, Doubling
The magician will be able to tell the answer after someone changes a secret number five times.

Trick 3. Number Split: Addition, Subtraction, Doubling, Halving
The magician will be able to tell the answer after someone changes a secret number six times.

Trick 4. Line 'Em Up: Drawing Parallel Lines**
The magician demonstrates how parallel lines can be drawn different ways.

Trick 5. Changeover: Addition, Subtraction, Halving, Doubling
A volunteer changes a number several times, but the magician knows the answer.

Trick 6. Flip 'Em: Addition, Subtraction**
Without looking, the magician will say what the sum of five numbers is after one has been changed.

Trick 7. Flip 'Em Backward: Addition, Subtraction**
This is the same as the previous trick done with different numbers.

Trick 8. Clock Opposites: Subtraction with Borrowing, Doubling, Addition
The magician correctly tells the answer after a volunteer finds the difference between the two numbers on a clock and changes it through doubling and halving.

Trick 9. Magic Toothpicks: Trickery**

This is not really a magic trick at all, but a play on words, which is fun for the performer and the audience.

Trick 10. Family Numbers: Addition, Doubling, Halving, Subtraction

The magician will be able to tell what the answer is after a volunteer has changed the number of members in his or her family through addition, subtraction, doubling, and halving.

Trick 11. Triple Trouble: Subtraction with Borrowing, Addition

A secret number is changed through reversing it and addition and subtraction, but the magician will be able to tell what the final answer is.

Trick 12. How Old Are You? Subtraction with Borrowing, Addition

The magician predicts the answer to a math problem that begins with a person's age.

Trick 13. Tricky Two-Step: Subtraction with Borrowing, Addition with Carrying

The magician predicts the final answer to a math problem after the original number has been changed through subtraction and addition.

Trick 14. Words and Numbers: Counting and Spelling**

The magician will predict the final number of a several step trick that involves counting and spelling.

Teacher Script

The first 14 magic tricks you will learn are tricks that you should perform only once each time you do your magic tricks. They are very simple tricks, great for warming up an audience, but the answer to each trick is always the same. If you perform them more than once, the audience will probably guess how the magic works and you want to keep that your secret.

Remember that each trick is followed by an explanation of what makes it work. After we learn each trick, but before we read that explanation, we'll take a few minutes to try to figure out the secret ourselves. It'll be fun to see if we can do that.

But don't worry. Even if you can figure it out, your audience will not be able to. That's because, when you perform magic tricks in a show, you don't give the audience time to think about anything. You perform one trick after another with very little time between tricks. Your magic secrets will be safe.

Now we're ready to begin to perform magic.

Magic Nines: Addition

Suggested introduction: **I will predict which pile of cards you will choose from three piles of cards.**

THE PROPS

three piles of cards taken from a deck of playing cards

THE TRICK

1. Before you start this trick, fix three piles of cards in this way:

   Pile 1 should have three nines.

   Piles 2 and 3 should have three cards that total 9. Example: 5, 2, 2 or 4, 3, 2

2. Ask someone to choose a pile of cards and say: **In my mind I can already see what pile you will pick. You will pick the nines pile.**

3. If he or she picks pile 1, he or she will see that it is a pile of nines. If he or she picks pile 2 or pile 3, add the cards to show they total 9 and prove that he or she chose a nines pile!

Do not let the volunteer see the other two piles or he or she will guess what the secret to this trick is.

THE MAGIC

Why does this work?

This trick is just plain trickery. You have fixed the cards so no matter what pile is picked it will always be a nines pile.

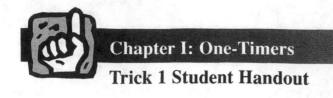

Magic Nines: Addition

Name _____ Date _____

Now you try it:

1. Fix three piles of cards so that one pile has three nines and two piles each have three cards that add up to 9.

2. Ask someone to choose one pile.

3. Did they choose a nines pile? Of course they did. They are all nines piles!

How did you do?

Materials (What props did you use?)

Procedure (How did you do the trick?)

Conclusion (What makes the magic work?)

Equations (What equations did you use to make the magic work?)

Halfies: Addition, Subtraction, Halving, Doubling

Suggested introduction: **After you choose a number and change it five times, I will tell you the number you end up with!**

THE PROPS

large piece of paper, dark-colored marker

THE TRICK

1. Put your blindfold on. Ask someone to pick any *even* number and write it on the paper.
2. Say: **Double your number.**
3. Say: **Add 12.**
4. Say: **Split your answer in half.**
5. Say: **Now split that number in half.**
6. Say: **Subtract half of the number you started with.**
7. Say some magic words and then say: **You have ended up with the number 3.**

THE MAGIC

If the steps are followed exactly as you read them, the answer to this puzzle will always be 3.

Why does this work?

Remember that doubling a number and then cutting it in half brings you right back to the number you started with. In this trick you start with any *even* number and double it. Then you add 12. When you split the answer in half, you get half of 12 which is 6 and half the number that was picked. Then you split the answer in half again. Now you end up with 3 (half of 6 is 3) and half of the number the volunteer picked. When he or she subtracts half of his or her number he or she is left with 3.

Example:

Pick 10.	10
Double it.	20
Add 12.	32
Split it in half.	16
Split it in half again.	8
Subtract half your original number.	$8 - 5 = 3$

The answer is 3, just as you said!

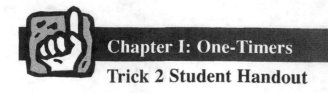

Halfies:
Addition, Subtraction,
Halving, Doubling

Name _____ Date _____

Now you try it:

1. Pick an *even* number.
2. Double it.
3. Add 12.
4. Split it in half.
5. Split the answer in half again.
6. Subtract half of the *even* number you picked.
7. If you followed the steps in order, your answer is 3.

How did you do?

Materials (What props did you use?)

Procedure (How did you do the trick?)

Conclusion (What makes the magic work?)

Equations (What equations did you use to make the trick work?)

Number Split:
Addition, Subtraction,
Doubling, Halving

Suggested introduction: **I will be able to tell you the number you end up with after you pick a number and change it in six ways.**

THE PROPS

large piece of paper, dark-colored marker

THE TRICK

1. Ask someone to pick a number and write it on the paper.
2. Say: **Double your number.**
3. Say: **Add 5.**
4. Say: **Now add 12.**
5. Say: **Subtract 3.**
6. Say: **Split the answer in half.**
7. Say: **Subtract the number you started with.**
8. Say some magic words and then tell them the answer. It will always be 7.

THE MAGIC

Remember doubling a number and then splitting it in half always gives you the number you started with.

Why does this work?

In this trick, you have someone double a number and then split it in half. That brings back the number he or she picked in the first place. When that number is subtracted, the volunteer is left with half of the numbers you gave him or her. Half of those numbers is 7.

Example:

Pick 7.	7
Double it.	14
Add 5.	19
Add 12.	31
Subtract 3.	28
Split in half.	14
Subtract the number you started with.	$14 - 7 = 7$

Follow the steps in order and the answer will always be 7.

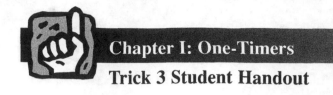
Number Split: Addition, Subtraction, Doubling, Halving

Name _____ Date _____

Now you try it:

1. Pick a number.
2. Double it.
3. Add 5.
4. Add 12.
5. Subtract 3.
6. Split the number in half.
7. Subtract the number you started with.
8. Your answer is 7.

How did you do?

Materials (What props did you use?)

Procedure (How did you do the trick?)

Conclusion (What makes the magic work?)

Equations (What equations did you use to make the magic work?)

Line 'Em Up: Drawing Parallel Lines

Suggested introduction: **Parallel lines are lines that are always the same distance from each other and always stay that way. I know two magic ways to draw parallel lines a different way.**

THE PROPS

large piece of paper

dark-colored marker

THE TRICK

1. Remind the audience what parallel lines look like by drawing two on the paper.

   Example: _____

   _____

2. Ask: **Does anyone here know a different way to draw lines that stay parallel to each other?**

3. Draw or show the audience a picture showing how parallel lines can stay the same distance from each other and still cross. Use the pictures below to help you.

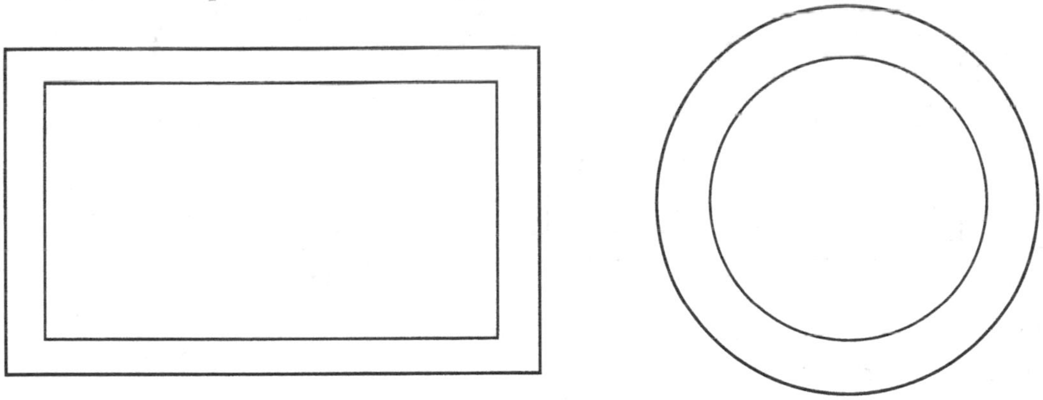

Figure 1.1 Parallel lines in a box and a circle.

THE MAGIC

When people think about parallel lines they think of straight lines that are the same distance from each other and never meet. They usually do not think of parallel lines that meet and change direction.

Why does this work?

As long as your lines stay the same distance from each other, they are parallel. If you are challenged that your round lines are not parallel lines, show them the parallel lines on a globe!

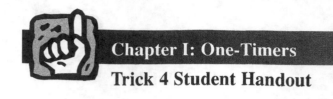

Line 'Em Up: Drawing Parallel Lines

Name _____ Date _____

Parallel lines are lines that are always the same distance from each other like the two stripes that run down the middle of a road.

_____

_____

Are there any ways to draw parallel lines differently? Yes, there are and you know the secret.

Now you try it:

Ask someone if he or she knows different ways to draw parallel lines. When the volunteer can't do it, draw a circle and a rectangle with parallel lines or show him or her the drawings below. They are examples of parallel lines because the lines stay the same distance from each other all the time.

How did you do?

Materials (What props did you use?)

Procedure (How did you do the trick?)

Conclusion (What makes the magic work?)

Changeover:
Addition, Subtraction,
Halving, Doubling

Suggested introduction: **You will choose a number and change it, but I will be able to tell you the answer you end up with.**

THE PROPS

large piece of paper

dark-colored marker

THE TRICK

1. Give someone the marker and put on your blindfold.
2. Say: **Write a number on the paper and add 3 to it.**
3. Say: **Double that number.**
4. Say: **Subtract 4.**
5. Say: **Split the answer in half.**
6. Say: **Subtract the number you picked in the first place.**
7. Say some magic words and tell the answer. It will always be 1 in this trick.

THE MAGIC

Doubling a number and then splitting it in half brings you back to the number you started with.

Why does this work?

You are asking someone to double a number and then split it in half. You know that will bring back the number that was picked in the first place. Then that number is subtracted too. All that is left are the numbers you gave. Those numbers get split in half too. Three doubled is 6. Six minus 4 leaves 2. Two split in half leaves 1.

    Example:

Pick 9.	9
Add 3.	12
Double it.	24
Subtract 4.	20
Split it in half.	10
Subtract the first number.	$10 - 9 = 1$

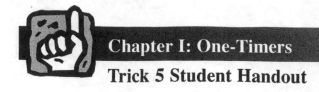

Changeover:
Addition, Subtraction,
Halving, Doubling

Name _____ Date _____

Now you try it:

1. Pick a number.
2. Add 3.
3. Double the answer.
4. Subtract 4.
5. Split the answer in half.
6. Subtract the number you picked in the first place.
7. The answer is 1.

How did you do?

Materials (What props did you use?)

Procedure (How did you do the trick?)

Conclusion (What makes the magic work?)

Equations (What equations did you use to make the magic work?)

Flip 'Em: Addition, Subtraction

Suggested introduction: **In this trick I will show that I don't have to look at numbers to add them and get the right answer.**

THE PROPS

- Five strips of paper about six inches long and one inch wide.
- On the first piece of paper, write 1 on one side.
  Turn it over and write 2 on the other side.
- On the next piece of paper, write 3 on one side
  and 4 on the other side.
- On the next piece of paper, write 5 on one side
  and 6 on the other side.
- Do the same for the numbers 7 and 8, and 9 and 10.

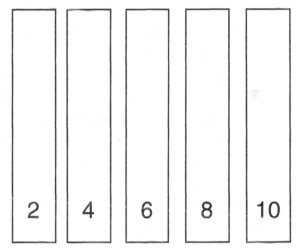

Figure 1.2 Strips of Paper with Even Numbers Showing

THE TRICK

1. Tape the papers to a wall or chart so the audience can see them with only the *even* numbers (2, 4, 6, 8, 10) showing. The numbers showing add up to 30.
2. Give a volunteer a small piece of tape and put on a blindfold or turn your back so you cannot see the papers.
3. Say to the volunteer: **Please turn over one piece of paper and tape it again to the wall. Add the numbers you see on all the slips of paper. Let me know when you're ready, but don't tell me the answer.**
4. When the volunteer is ready, say: **Even though I can't see which piece of paper you have turned over, I can tell you the sum of all the numbers.**
5. Say some magic words and pretend you are thinking very hard. Then announce that the sum of your numbers is 29.

THE MAGIC

The answer in this trick will always be 29.

Why does this work?

The numbers showing on the papers total 30. The number on the backside of each slip of paper is one less than the number on top. So no matter which strip of paper is turned over, the answer will always be one less than 30. It's simple subtraction. One less than 30 is, of course, 29 (30 − 1 = 29).

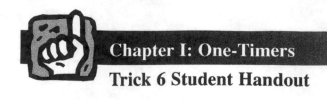
Flip 'Em: Addition, Subtraction

Name _____ Date _____

Now you try it:

1. Fix five strips of paper so that *even* numbers are written on one side and *odd* numbers on the reverse side. The numerals 1 and 2 are on the same paper, 3 and 4 on another, 5 and 6 on another, 7 and 8 on another, and, 9 and 10 on the last.

2. Lay out the five pieces of paper with the *even* numbers 2, 4, 6, 8 and 10 showing.

3. Add the numbers. You should reach the sum of 30.

4. Turn over one piece of paper to show the *odd* number written on the other side.

5. Is the sum of the numbers now 29? It has to be because numbers always work in a logical manner, and one less than 30 is 29.

How did you do?

Materials (What props did you use?)

Procedure (How did you do the trick?)

Conclusion (What makes the trick work?)

Equations (What equations did you use to make the trick work?)

Flip 'Em Backward: Addition, Subtraction

Suggested introduction: **To show I really can add numbers without looking at them, I'll do it again.**

THE PROPS

Use the same numbered slips of paper you used in Trick 6. But this time use the reverse side so the *odd* numbers show. Remember, 1 and 2 are on the same paper, 3 and 4 on another, 5 and 6 on another, 7 and 8 on another, and 9 and 10 on the last.

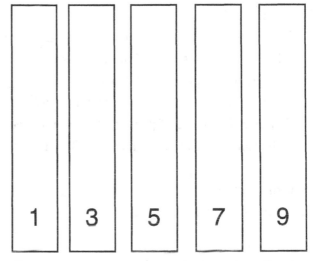

Figure 1.3 Strips of Paper with Odd Numbers Showing

THE TRICK

1. Tape the slips of paper to the wall or chart just the way you did for the last trick, only this time let the *odd* numbers show (1, 3, 5, 7, 9). The sum of the numbers should be 25.
2. Give the volunteer a small piece of tape and turn your back or put on your blindfold.
3. Say: **Turn over one piece of paper and tape it again to the wall. Add the numbers you see. Tell me when you are ready, but do not tell me the answer.**
4. When the volunteer tells you he or she is ready, say: **Even though I cannot see what you have done, I will tell you the sum of the numbers.**
5. Say some magic words. Then announce that the answer is 26.

THE MAGIC

The answer to this trick will always be 26.

Why does this work?

The sum of the *odd* numbers is 25. The bottom numbers on each paper are 1 more than the numbers that are on top. No matter which paper is turned over, 1 more will be added. The answer will always be 1 more than 25, which is 26 (1 + 25 = 26).

Flip 'Em Backward: Addition, Subtraction

Name _____ Date _____

Now you try it:

1. Fix five pieces of paper so that *even* numbers are written on one side and *odd* numbers on the reverse side. The numerals 1 and 2 are on the same paper, 3 and 4 on another, 5 and 6 on another, 7 and 8 on another, and 9 and 10 on the last.
2. Lay out the five pieces of paper with the *odd* numbers 1, 3, 5, 7, and 9 showing.
3. Turn over one piece of paper so the *even* number written on the other side shows.
4. Is the sum of the numbers now 26? Of course it is. Remember, numbers work in a logical way.

How did you do?

Materials (What props did you use?)

Procedure (How did you do the trick?)

Conclusion (What makes the trick work?)

Equations (What equations did you use to make the trick work?)

Clock Opposites: Subtraction with Borrowing, Doubling, Addition

Suggested introduction: **I will get the right answer to the work you do with numbers from a clock, even though you will not tell me what number you start with.**

THE PROPS

dark-colored marker

clock or a drawing of a clock

large piece of paper posted where the audience can see it

Figure 1.4 Opposite Numbers on a Clock Face

THE TRICK

1. Ask for a volunteer and show him or her the clock, then turn your back.
2. Say: **Please choose two opposite numbers on the clock and write them on the paper.**
3. Say: **Subtract the smaller number from the larger. Then add 10.**
4. Say: **Now double your answer.**
5. Say: **Now subtract 5 from your answer and tell me when you are ready.**
6. When the volunteer has the answer, say some magic words and tell him or her the answer is 27.

THE MAGIC

Because you know that the difference between opposite numbers on a clock is always 6, it's easy to get the answer to this trick.

Why does this work?

There are 12 hours on the clock. Opposite numbers are half of the clock away from each other so they are half of 12, which is 6. You know the number they start with! Then the volunteer adds and subtracts numbers you give him or her so you are always in control of what the answer will be. The answer is always 27 in this trick if you use the numbers given. If you decide to change the numbers, figure out what the new answer will be before you do the trick.

Example:

When the volunteer subtracts the two opposite numbers his or her answer will be 6.

Then 10 is added.	$6 + 10 = 16$
That answer is doubled	$16 + 16 = 32$
The last step is to subtract 5.	$32 - 5 = 27$

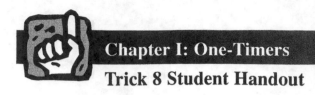
Clock Opposites: Subtraction with Borrowing, Doubling, Addition

Name _____ Date _____

Look at all the opposite numbers on the clock:

12 is opposite 6; 1 is opposite 7; 2 is opposite 8; 3 is opposite 9; 4 is opposite 10; 5 is opposite 11; and 6 is opposite 12. Is the difference between each pair of numbers always 6? Yes, it is, because the numbers are halfway around the clock from each other, which is half of 12, or 6.

Now you try it:

1. Choose two numbers on the clock and subtract the smaller one from the larger one.
2. Add 10 and double your answer.
3. Subtract 5. Is the answer 27?

Figure 1.4 Opposite Numbers on a Clock Face

How did you do?

Materials (What props did you use?)

Procedure (How did you do the trick?)

Conclusion (What makes the trick work?)

Equations (What equations did you use to make the trick work?)

Magic Toothpicks: Trickery

This is a trick that isn't magical, but it's fun to do anyway, just for laughs.

Suggested introduction: **I can change nine toothpicks into ten!**

THE PROPS

nine toothpicks

an overhead projector if you are performing the trick for a large audience

THE TRICK

1. Lay nine toothpicks in a row on a table or on an overhead projector.

2. Say to your audience: **Here are nine toothpicks. Can anyone here turn nine toothpicks into ten?**

3. When no one in your audience can do it, say some magic words while you show how it's done. (See the picture.)

THE MAGIC

You make the audience think you will make ten toothpicks out of nine, but you will make ten a different way!

Why does this work?

You move the toothpicks around so they spell the word *"ten"*. The picture shows you how.

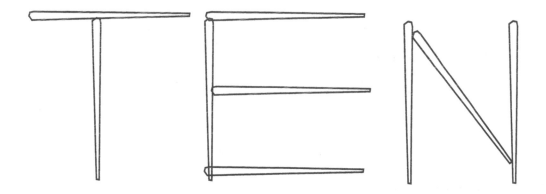

Figure 1.5 Arrangement of Toothpicks

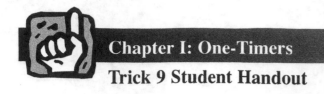

Magic Toothpicks: Trickery

Name _____ Date _____

Now you try it:

1. Place nine toothpicks on a table.

2. Arrange the nine toothpicks to spell the word *"ten"* just as it shows in the picture.

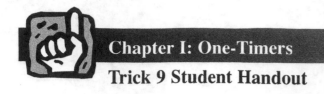

How did you do?

Materials (What props did you use?)

Procedure (How did you do the trick?)

Conclusion (What makes the trick work?)

Family Numbers: Addition, Doubling, Halving, Subtraction

Suggested introduction: **You are going to start with the number of people in your family and change the number several times. No matter what you do to the numbers, I will be able to tell what your final answer is.**

THE PROPS

large piece of paper, dark-colored marker

THE TRICK

1. Turn your back and ask a volunteer to write the number of people in his or her family on the paper.
2. Say: **Add the number 7.**
3. Say: **Double your answer.**
4. Say: **Now subtract 2.**
5. Say: **Split your answer in half.**
6. Say: **The last thing you will do is subtract the number of people in your family from the last answer.**
7. After you say your magic words, announce what the final answer is. It is 6.

THE MAGIC

This trick has nothing at all to do with how many people are in the volunteer's family.

That number is just used so that the audience will not guess what you are doing with the other numbers.

Why does this work?

Seven doubled is 14. You subtract 2 to get 12. Twelve split in half is 6. The volunteer adds the number of people in his or her family and then subtracts the number of people in his or her family. So you are always left with 6.

Example:

If there are 5 people in the family:

5 + 7 = 12

12 doubled is 24

24 − 2 = 22

22 split in half equals 11

11 − 5 = 6

Since you start with the number of family members and then subtract it, it does not change your answer, which will always be 6. The family member numbers are put in just to trick the audience.

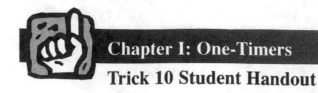

Family Numbers: Addition, Doubling, Halving, Subtraction

Name _____ Date _____

Now you try it:

1. Write down the number of people in your family.

2. Add 7 to that number.

3. Double your answer.

4. Then subtract 2.

5. Split that number in half.

6. Subtract the number of people in your family.

7. Your answer is 6, isn't it? Congratulations! You are a very good magician.

How did you do?

Materials (What props did you use?)

Procedure (How did you do the trick?)

Conclusion (What makes the trick work?)

Equations (What equations did you use to make the trick work?)

Triple Trouble:
Subtraction with Borrowing, Addition

Suggested introduction: **You are going to choose any number you want and change it by turning it around and adding and subtracting it, but you won't fool me. I will be able to tell you what your final answer is.**

PROPS

dark-colored marker, large piece of paper

THE TRICK

1. Put the paper where the audience can see what is being written on it.
2. Give the volunteer a marker and put on your blindfold.
3. Say: **Write three different numbers between 1 and 9 so that you have a three-digit number with the largest number first and the smallest number last.**

Example: 742

4. Say: **Reverse that three-digit number so that the smallest number is now first and the largest one is now last. Write that under the first number and subtract it from the top number.**

Example: 742 − 247 = 495

5. Say: **Now add the three digits in your answer.**

Example: 4 + 9 + 5

6. Without taking off your blindfold, say some magic words. Then announce that the answer is 18.

THE MAGIC

When a three-digit number is reversed and the smaller one subtracted from the larger one, the sum of the digits in the answer is always 18.

Why does this work?

When you reverse the numbers, the middle digit stays the same: 7<u>4</u>2 and 2<u>4</u>7.

But the final digit of the top number is smaller than the final digit of the bottom number.

$$742$$
$$- 247$$

So when you subtract, you will need to borrow. Because the middle number is the same on the top and the bottom, borrowing makes the middle digit in your answer come out as a 9.

$$742$$
$$- 247$$
$$495$$

The borrowing makes the other numbers in your answer total 9, too.

$$4 + 5 = 9$$

Since 9 plus 9 equals 18, you will always have the right answer handy.

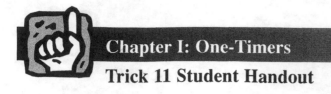

Triple Trouble:
Subtraction with Borrowing, Addition

Name _____ Date _____

Now you try it:

1. Write a three-digit number with the largest digit first and the smallest last.

    Example: 321

2. Reverse the number and subtract the smaller one from the larger one.

    Example: 321 – 123

3. Do the digits in your answer add up to 18? Of course they do. You are never wrong when you do math magic!

How did you do?

Materials (What props did you use?)

Procedure (How did you do the trick)

Conclusion (What makes the magic work?)

Equations (What equations did you use to make the trick work?)

How Old Are You?
Subtraction with Borrowing, Addition

Suggested introduction: **I will be able to predict the answer to a math problem even though we will start with your age, and I don't know how old you are.**

THE PROPS

dark-colored marker

small piece of paper

large piece of paper posted where the audience can see it

THE TRICK

1. Write the number 9 on a small piece of paper. Fold the paper and ask someone in the audience to hold it until you ask him or her to open it.
2. Say: **This is my prediction for the answer to this number problem.**
3. Ask for a volunteer who is *older than 13*. Tell the person not to tell you his or her age.
4. Say: **Write down your age, then reverse the digits and subtract the smaller number from the larger one.**
5. Say: **Add the two digits in the answer.**
6. Now ask the person in the audience to whom you gave the paper to unfold it and read your prediction out loud. Of course your prediction was correct!

THE MAGIC

This is another trick that works because you have to borrow when you subtract.

Why does this work?

When you reverse a number and subtract the smaller one from the bigger one, you will always have to borrow. When you subtract reversed numbers you will always get 9 or digits that add up to 9.

Example: 41 – 14 = 27 and 2 + 7 = 9

Note: This trick will not work if the person's age contains two numbers that are the same (22, 33, 55, and so on).

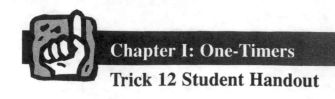
How Old Are You?
Subtraction with Borrowing, Addition

Name _____ Date _____

Now you try it:

1. Write down any age that is over 13 that does not contain the same two digits such as 22 or 55. Use the example as a guide, but try it yourself with a different number.

    Example: 25

2. Reverse it and subtract the smaller from the larger number.

    Example: 52 – 25 = 27

3. Add the two digits in the answer.

    Example: 2 + 7 = 9

4. Your answer is 9, right? Of course it is. You are never wrong!

How did you do?

Materials (What props did you use?)

Procedure (How did you do the trick?)

Conclusion (What makes the magic work?)

Equations (What equations did you use to make the trick work?)

Tricky Two-Step: Subtraction with Borrowing, Addition with Carrying

Suggested introduction: **I will predict the answer to the math problem you will do even though I do not know what numbers you will choose.**

THE PROPS

dark-colored marker

a small piece of paper

a large piece of paper hung where the audience can see it

THE TRICK

1. Write the number 1089 on a piece of paper and fold it. Don't reveal the number. Make a big show of folding the paper and giving it to a member of the audience to hold.
2. Say: **The number I have written on this paper is my prediction for the answer to the number problem we are going to do.**
3. Ask for a volunteer and give that person a marker.
4. Say: **Write down a three-digit number using three different digits. None of them can be a zero.**
5. Say: **Reverse the number and subtract the smaller one from the larger one.**
6. Say: **Now reverse the answer and add those two numbers.**

Example:

462 reverses to 264

462 − 264 = 198

198 reverses to 891

198 + 891 = 1089

7. Ask the person in the audience to open the paper and read out loud the prediction you wrote. Of course, you are correct! Take a deep bow. You deserve it!

THE MAGIC

This is another trick that because of borrowing will come out as you wish.

Why does this work?

Just as we did in Tricks 11 and 12, we asked the volunteer to reverse two numbers and subtract them. We know that the digits in the answer will all add up to 9. When the numbers are again reversed and this time added, the numbers in the ones column will always add up to 9, the two 9's in the center column will always add up to 18, and the final column (because you have to carry the 1) will add up to 10. You end up with 1089.

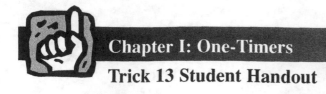
Tricky Two-Step: Subtraction with Borrowing, Addition with Carrying

Name _____ Date _____

Now you try it:

1. Write a three-digit number with no zeros in it. Use the example as a guide, but try it yourself with a different number.

Example: 447

2. Reverse the number and subtract the smaller number from the larger one.

Example: 744 – 447 = 297

3. Reverse that number and add it to the last answer.

Example: 792 + 297 = 1089

4. Is your answer 1089 just as it is in the example? It should be if you added and subtracted carefully.

How did you do?

Materials (What props did you use?)

Procedure (How did you do the trick?)

Conclusion (What makes the magic work?)

Equations (What equations did you use to make the trick work?)

Words and Numbers: Counting and Spelling

Suggested introduction: **This is a spelling and math trick, but I will still be able to predict what your final number will be.**

THE PROPS

dark-colored marker

small piece of paper

large piece of paper posted where the audience can see it

THE TRICK

1. Choose a volunteer and say: **You are going to pick a secret number and change it in several ways. But before you do that, I am going to predict your final number.**
2. Take a piece of paper and write the number 4 on it. Don't let anyone see the number you wrote.
3. Fold the paper and give it to someone in the audience to hold. Say: **This is my prediction. Please hold this paper until the trick is over.**
4. Say to the volunteer: **Please choose a number and write it on the paper. You are going to have to spell the number you wrote so make sure you pick a number you can spell.**
5. When the number is written, say: **Now write the word for your number.**
6. Say: **Count the letters in the word you have written and write that number down.**
7. Say: **It's spelling time again. Write the word for your last number.**
8. Say: **Now count the letters in that word and write that number.**
9. Repeat these two steps until the volunteer writes the number 4, the number you predicted.
10. Say: **Would the person who is holding my prediction please stand and read what number I predicted?**
11. When the number 4 is read, take your bow.

THE MAGIC

The answer in this trick will always be 4.

Why does this work?

The word "*four*" is the only word that has exactly the same number of letters as the number it represents. No matter which number is chosen as the first number in this series, 4 is the only possible last number.

Example:

35

thirty-five

10

ten

3

three

5

five

4

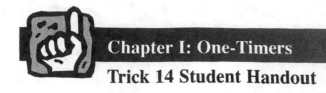

Words and Numbers: Counting and Spelling

Name _____ Date _____

Now you try it:

1. Pick a number, any number, but make sure you can spell it!
2. Write the number.
3. Write the word for that number.
4. Count how many letters are in the word and write that number.
5. Keep going until you reach the number 4.

How did you do?

Materials (What props did you use?)

Procedure (How did you do the trick?)

Conclusion (What makes the trick work?)

Chapter II
CALENDAR CAPERS

✳ ✳ ✳ ✳ ✳ ✳ ✳ ✳ ✳ ✳ ✳

Teacher Notes

The tricks in this chapter use many of the same processes to make the magic work as those in Chapter I. One of the tricks, however, works because the numbers on a calendar are in numerical order and evenly spaced and are seven numbers apart vertically and one number apart horizontally.

    The math is just addition and subtraction, halving and doubling.

Trick 15. What's the Date? Addition, Subtraction, Doubling, Halving
The magician will be able to tell what date someone has chosen from the calendar.

Trick 16. Calendar Opposites: Addition with Carrying, Doubling
The magician will add four pairs of opposite numbers on a calendar without knowing what the numbers are.

Trick 17. When Were You Born? Addition with Carrying, Subtraction, Doubling
The magician will be able to name someone's birth month.

Trick 18. The Very Day: Addition with Carrying, Subtraction, Doubling
The magician can even name the very date of someone's birth.

Teacher Script

Calendars are a great prop to use for some very puzzling magic tricks. That's because calendars are arranged in a very orderly fashion. The numbers are in number order and numbers above and below each other are exactly seven numbers apart. (*Demonstrate these facts on a calendar.*)

What did we do to make it seem as if there were three numbers all the same instead of three evenly spaced numbers? We subtracted the difference between the numbers from the largest number and added it to the smallest number. (*Demonstrate or have a student show how the process is done using numbers from a calendar.*) Knowing how to do this is going to help us do a very tricky trick.

The tricks we are going to learn will be easy for you to do but they will amaze your audience. All we will use for these tricks is a calendar large enough so that the audience can read the numbers. We will be able to tell what date someone picks from the calendar, add opposite numbers on a calendar after only being told the first number, and guess correctly the month and date of someone's birthday.

What's the Date?
Addition, Subtraction, Doubling, Halving

Suggested introduction: **Without looking, I will be able to tell what date you pick from a calendar.**

THE PROPS

crayon

page from a calendar

THE TRICK

1. Give a volunteer the calendar page and the crayon.
2. Turn your back or put your blindfold on.
3. Say: **Pick and circle any date.**
4. Say: **Double the number.**
5. Say: **Add 4.**
6. Say: **Split that number in half and tell me the answer.**
7. Subtract 2 from the number he or she gives you and you will have the number chosen from the calendar.

THE MAGIC

All you have to do in this trick is ask someone to double the number he or she chose from the calendar, add 4, then split the answer in half. When you subtract 2 from the answer you have the number that is circled.

Why does this work?

The volunteer doubles his or her number and splits it in half. That brings him or her back to the number he or she chose in the first place. He or she adds 4 and splits that in half too. Half of 4 is 2. So the final answer is his or her number plus 2. When you subtract 2 from the answer he or she gives you, you are left with the number he or she picked in the first place.

Example:

Circle the number 15.

Double the number: $15 + 15 = 30$ or $2 \times 15 = 30$.

Add 4: $30 + 4 = 34$.

Split that number in half. Half of 34 is 17.

$17 - 2 = 15$, the number circled in step 1.

What's the Date?
Addition, Subtraction, Doubling, Halving

Name _____ Date _____

Now you try it:

1. Choose a date on the calendar.
2. Double the number.
3. Add 4.
4. Split the answer in half.
5. Subtract 2 to get the number you circled.

How did you do?

Materials (What props did you use?)

Procedure (How did you do the trick?)

Conclusion (What makes the magic work?)

Equations (What equations did you use to make the trick work?)

MAY						
					1	2
3	4	5	6	7	8	9
10	11	12	13	14	15	16
17	18	19	20	21	22	23
24	25	26	27	28	29	30
31						

Calendar Opposites:
Addition with Carrying, Doubling

Suggested introduction: **I will add four pairs of opposite numbers on a calendar without knowing what the numbers are.**

THE PROPS

a few pieces of transparent tape

calendar showing one month taped or hung where the audience can see it

piece of paper with a box cut out to show three rows of three numbers each when placed over the calendar

Figure 2.1 Calendar Setup

THE TRICK

1. Hang the calendar where the audience can see it and give the cutout paper to a volunteer. Then put on your blindfold.
2. Say: **Tape the paper anywhere over the calendar so three rows of three numbers show. Tell me the first number in the box, and I will tell you the sum of each pair of opposite numbers in the box.**
3. As soon as the person tells you the first number, add 8 to it. Then double the answer. That number will be the sum of each pair of opposite numbers.
4. Say some magic words and tell your audience what your answer is.
5. Ask someone to add all the opposite pairs to prove you are right. Don't worry, you will be!

THE MAGIC

Because there are seven days in a week, numbers above and below each other on a calendar are always seven numbers apart. Adding 8 to the first number brings you one row down and one space over to the center number of the square. Once you know the center number, you double it because the center number doubled is the sum of each pair of opposite numbers.

Why does this work?

Adding 8 to the first number in a box brings you one row down and one space over to the center number of the square.

Once you know the center number, you double it because the center number doubled is the sum of each pair of opposite numbers.

Example:

In a calendar box showing

7	8	9
14	15	16
21	22	23

7 is the first number.

7 + 8 = 15, the center number of the square, and 15 doubled is 30.

Look at the opposites numbers and add them.

7 + 23 = 30, 8 + 22 = 30, 9 + 21 = 30, and 14 + 16 = ? Is it 30?

Yes, it is, because doubling the middle number of the square will always give you the sum of the opposite numbers!

Calendar Opposites:
Addition with Carrying, Doubling

Name _____ Date _____

Now you try it:

1. On the calendar page shown, choose and circle any box of three numbers down and three numbers across.
2. Add 8 to the first number in the box and then double that number.
3. Is your answer the sum of each pair of opposite numbers? It absolutely, positively should be!

February ♥ ♥						
1	2	3	4	5	6	7
8	9	10	11	12	13	14
15	16	17	18	19	20	21
22	23	24	25	26	27	28
29						

How did you do?

Materials (What props did you use?)

Procedure (How did you do the trick?)

Conclusion (What makes the magic work?)

Equations (What equations did you use to make the trick work?)

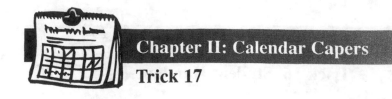

When Were You Born? Addition with Carrying, Subtraction, Doubling

Suggested introduction: **I am going to be able to tell you in what month you were born.**

PROPS

dark-colored marker

calendar with the months numbered 1 through 12, with January as number 1 and December as number 12

THE TRICK

1. Give a volunteer the marker and put on your blindfold.
2. Say: **Look through the calendar and pick out your birthday month.**
3. Say: **Write the number of the month.**
4. Say: **Add the number of the month five times (or multiply it by 5).**
5. Say: **Add 6 to that answer.**
6. Say: **Double that number and tell me the answer.**
7. In your head, subtract 12 from the number you are given. Your answer will have a zero in the ones column. Cross out the zero. Say some magic words and tell the volunteer the month when he or she was born. It will be the number or numbers you are left with.

THE MAGIC

If you follow the steps of this trick in exact order, the number or numbers in your final answer after you cross out the zero in the ones column will be the month of the volunteer's birthday.

Why does this work?

When the volunteer adds his or her number five times and then doubles it, he or she ends up with his or her number with a zero after it. It is like adding his or her number ten times or multiplying it by 10. (Try it and see. Add 2 ten times: 2, 4, 6, 8, 10, 12, 14, 16, 18, 20. You end up with the number 2 with a zero after it.) Then 6 is added and doubled. Six doubled is 12. When you subtract 12 from the last number, you get the volunteer's number (birth month) with a zero after it. Cross out the zero and you have his or her number (birth month).

Example:

Birthday month is May, the 5th month.	$5 + 5 + 5 + 5 + 5 = 25$ (5 x 5 = 25)
Add 6.	$25 + 6 = 31$
Double the answer.	$31 + 31 = 62$
In your head subtract 12 and you end up with 50.	$62 - 12 = 50$

Cross out the zero and you have 5, the number for the 5th month of the year, May.

When Were You Born? Addition with Carrying, Subtraction, Doubling

Name _____ Date _____

Here's a numbered listing of the months of the year to use when you do this trick.

January 1	February 2	March 3
April 4	May 5	June 6
July 7	August 8	September 9
October 10	November 11	December 12

Now you try it:

1. Turn to the month on a calendar when you were born and write the number of that month on the paper. Add the number five times.
2. Add 6 and double the answer.
3. Subtract 12. You should have the month of your birth with a zero after it. Cross out the zero and you are done.

How did you do?

Materials (What props did you use?)

Procedure (How did you do the trick?)

Conclusion (What makes the magic work?)

Equations (What equations did you use to make the trick work?)

The Very Day: Addition with Carrying, Subtraction, Doubling

Suggested introduction: **I am going to tell you the number of the day when you were born.**

PROPS

calendar, dark-colored marker

THE TRICK

1. Give a volunteer the marker and put on your blindfold.
2. Say: **Write the number of the day when you were born.**
3. Say: **Add that number five times (or multiply it by 5).**
4. Say: **Add 7 to that answer.**
5. Say: **Double that number and tell me the answer.**
6. In your head, subtract 14 from the number you are given. Your answer will have a zero in the ones column. Cross out the zero. Say some magic words and tell the volunteer the number of the day when he or she was born. It will be the number or numbers you are left with.

THE MAGIC

If you follow the steps of this trick in exact order, the number or numbers in your final answer after you cross out the zero in the ones column will be the date of the volunteer's birthday.

Why does this work?

When the volunteer adds his or her number five times and then doubles it, he or she ends up with his or her number with a zero after it. It is like adding his or her number ten times or multiplying it by 10. (Try it and see. Add 2 ten times: 2, 4, 6, 8, 10, 12, 14, 16, 18, 20. You end up with the number 2 with a zero after it.) Then 7 is added and doubled. Seven doubled is 14. When you subtract 14 from the last number, you get the volunteer's number (birth date) with a zero after it. Cross out the zero and you have his or her number (birth date).

Example:

He or she was born on the 25th day of the month.	$25 + 25 + 25 + 25 + 25 = 125$
Add 7.	$125 + 7 = 132$
Double the answer.	$132 + 132 = 264$
Subtract 14.	$264 - 14 = 250$

Cross out the zero and you have the date of the day when the volunteer was born. He or she was born on the 25th day of the month.

The Very Day: Addition with Carrying, Subtraction, Doubling

Name _____ Date _____

Now you try it:

1. Write the number of the day when you were born.
2. Add the number 5 times.
3. Add 7.
4. Double the answer.
5. Subtract 14. You should have the date of your birth with a zero after it. Cross out the zero and you are done.

How did you do?

Materials (What props did you use?)

Procedure (How did you do the trick?)

Conclusion (What makes the magic work?)

Equations (What equations did you use to make the trick work?)

Chapter III
DICE DOINGS
✳ ✳ ✳ ✳ ✳ ✳ ✳ ✳ ✳ ✳ ✳
Teacher Notes

Ordinary dice are used for all four tricks in this chapter. The math and reasoning in all the tricks is not difficult, but the first and last tricks are especially easy.

Trick 19. Transparent Dice: Addition and Subtraction**

The magician will be able to add the numbers on the bottoms of dice without looking at them. Although this trick calls for four dice, it works with any number of dice, and instructions are given at the end of the trick for changing the number of dice used.

Trick 20. Crazy Eight: Addition with Carrying, Subtraction with Borrowing, Doubling

Without looking, the magician will be able to tell what two numbers have been rolled on a pair of dice.

Trick 21. Roll 'Em Partner: Addition, Subtraction, Doubling, Halving

A number is rolled on the die and is changed by doubling, and addition and subtraction, and the magician will say what the answer is.

Trick 22. I've Got Your Number: Doubling, Halving, Addition, Subtraction**

The magician will be able to tell what number is rolled on one die. This trick can also be done without a die, so it's like having two tricks in one. Do it once with a die and once having a volunteer pick a number. It works equally well either way.

✳ ✳ ✳ ✳ ✳ ✳ ✳ ✳ ✳ ✳ ✳
Teacher Script

You've probably played a lot of games where you used dice. Well, in the next few tricks you will be using dice again, but this time you will be performing magic tricks with the dice. The dice will be ordinary ones, just like you use in your games, but the tricks won't be ordinary at all.

You will be able to add the numbers on the bottoms of dice without seeing them, tell what one or two numbers have been rolled, and know what the answer is after a number has been changed in several ways.

Some of the following tricks call for using paper and marker. Just as you did in some of the tricks you've already learned, you should have the volunteer do his or her work on a large piece of paper that the audience can see.

Now it's time to toss those little white cubes and see what magic we can roll!

Transparent Dice: Addition and Subtraction

Suggested introduction: **I will add the numbers on the bottom of the dice even though I can't see them!**

THE PROPS
four dice

THE TRICK

1. Ask a volunteer to toss the four dice on the table.
2. Say: **With my magical powers, I am able to see through the dice. I will add the numbers on the bottom of these dice, even though I cannot see them.**
3. In your head, add the numbers on the top of the dice and subtract that number from 28. Say some magic words and tell them what the answer is.
4. Ask the volunteer to turn over the dice, one at a time, and add the bottom numbers out loud so the audience can hear. The sum will be the number you have named!

THE MAGIC

If you use four dice, all you have to do is subtract the sum of the numbers on the top of the dice from 28 to find the sum of the numbers on the bottom of the dice.

Why does this work?

When you add the number on the top and bottom on any one die, the answer will be seven. If you have four dice, that is 4 times 7, or 28. Twenty-eight is the sum of the top and bottom numbers on all four dice. By subtracting the sum of the top numbers from 28, you will always come out with the sum of the bottom numbers.

> **Example:**
>
> If the sum of the top numbers on the dice equals 11, then 28 – 11 = 17, which is what the bottom numbers will add up to.

*You can use any number of dice you like. Just remember that the sum of the top and bottom numbers on each die equals 7. If you use *two dice*, the sum of the top and bottom numbers will be 14 so you subtract the sum of the top numbers from 14. If you use *three dice*, the sum of the top and bottom numbers will be 21 so you will subtract the sum of the top numbers from 21.

Transparent Dice:
Addition and Subtraction

Name _____ Date _____

Now you try it:

1. Roll four dice and add the numbers that are on top.
2. Subtract your answer from 28 and write that number down.
3. Then add up the numbers on the bottoms of the dice.
4. Is it the same number you arrived at when you did your subtraction? Of course it is. This trick will always work for you. When you add the number on the top and bottom of any one die, the answer will be 7. You used four dice and four 7's are 28. You subtract the sum of the top numbers from 28. This gives you the sum of the bottom numbers.

How did you do?

Materials (What props did you use?)

Procedure (How did you do the trick?)

Conclusion (What makes the magic work?)

Equations (What equations did you use to make the trick work?)

Crazy Eight: Addition with Carrying, Subtraction with Borrowing, Doubling

Suggested introduction: **I won't look, but I will know what two numbers come up when you roll dice!**

THE PROPS

two dice

large piece of paper

dark-colored marker

THE TRICK

1. Put the paper where the audience can see it, and give a volunteer the dice and marker.
2. Turn your back or use your blindfold.
3. Say: **Roll two dice and write down the numbers.**
4. Say: **Pick one of the numbers and add it five times (multiply it by 5).**
5. Say: **Add 8 to the answer.**
6. Say: **Now double that number.**
7. Say: **Now add the number on the other die and tell me the answer.**
8. In your head, subtract 16 from the number the person tells you, and then tell the person the two digits in your answer. They will be the two numbers the volunteer rolled.

THE MAGIC

When you add one of the numbers five times, double the answer, and add the other number, you end up with the two numbers rolled. You use the number 8 to confuse the audience.

Why does this work?

This works because when you add a number five times and then double it you end up with the number followed by a zero.

> **Example:** Let's say 3 was the number on the die that the volunteer chose.
>
> Add it 5 times. $3 + 3 + 3 + 3 + 3 = 15$
>
> Double the answer. 15 doubled is 30
>
> You end up with the 3 with a zero after it.

When you add the number from the second die, it takes the place of the zero so you now have the two numbers that were rolled. The 8 is added just to fool the audience. You add 8 to the number, then have the volunteer double the answer in the next step. Eight doubled is 16, so when you subtract 16, you are just taking out was put in.

Crazy Eight: Addition with Carrying, Subtraction with Borrowing, Doubling

Name _____ Date _____

Now you try it:

1. Roll two dice. Write the two numbers you rolled.

2. Pick one of the numbers and add it 5 times.

3. Add 8 to the answer.

4. Double the answer.

5. Add the number on the other die.

6. Subtract 16 from your answer. Did you end up with the two numbers you rolled in the first place?

How did you do?

Materials (What props did you use?)

Procedure (How did you do the trick?)

Conclusion (What makes the magic work?)

Equations (What equations did you use to make this trick work?)

Roll 'Em, Partner:
Addition, Subtraction, Doubling, Halving

Suggested introduction: **After you roll a number and change it by doubling it and adding and subtracting other numbers, I will tell you what your answer is without looking.**

THE PROPS

dark-colored marker

large piece of paper

one die

THE TRICK

1. Put the paper where the audience can see it and give a volunteer the marker.
2. Turn your back or put on your blindfold.
3. Say: **I am going to ask you to do some work with numbers. Please use the paper and marker to help you follow my directions.**
4. Say: **Roll the die and write the number you rolled. Double the number.**
5. Now, in your head, *you* pick an *even* number between 2 and 10 (2, 4, 6, 8, 10).
   (IMPORTANT: Be sure to remember this number!)
   Say: **Add_____ (the number you picked) to your answer.**
6. Say: **Now split your new answer in half.**
7. Say: **Subtract the number that you rolled on the die.**
8. Say some magic words and tell the answer. It will be half the *even* number you gave in step five.

THE MAGIC

The answer will always be one half of the *even* number you chose in step five.

Why does this work?

This works because when the volunteer doubles the number on the die and splits it in half, he or she ends up with the number on the die.

Example:

Two doubled is 4.

Half of 4 is 2.

So when the volunteer subtracts his or her number from the answer in step 7, all he or she has left is half of the number you gave him or her.

Roll 'Em, Partner:
Addition, Subtraction, Doubling, Halving

Name _____ Date _____

Now you try it:

1. Roll one die. Write the number you rolled.
2. Double the number.
3. Pick an even number from 2 through 10 and add it to the answer.
4. Divide the new answer in half.
5. Subtract the number you rolled.
6. The answer will always be half of the even number you choose. Simple as can be when you know what you're doing. Right?

How did you do?

Materials (What props did you use?)

Procedure (How did you do the trick?)

Conclusion (What makes the magic work?)

Equations (What equations did you use to make the trick work?)

I've Got Your Number:
Doubling, Halving, Addition, Subtraction

Suggested introduction: **Without looking, I will correctly guess what number you roll on one die.**

THE PROPS

one die

piece of paper

dark-colored marker

THE TRICK

1. Put the paper where the audience can see it and give a volunteer the marker and a die.

2. Turn your back on the volunteer or put on your blindfold.

3. Say: **Roll a number and write it on the piece of paper. Don't tell me what you wrote.**

4. Say: **Double the number you rolled and add 2 to the answer.**

5. Say: **Divide that number in half and tell me your final answer.**

6. You will subtract 1 from the volunteer's answer to get the number he or she started with.

7. Announce that number and take a deep bow.

THE MAGIC

All you have to do in this trick is ask someone to double the number he or she rolled on one die, add 2, then divide the answer by 2. You subtract 1 from the answer he or she tells you, and you will know what number he or she rolled.

Why does this work?

When the volunteer doubles his or her number and then divides it by 2, he or she is really doubling it and then splitting it in half. This gives the volunteer the number he or she rolled in the first place! This is like walking the same number of steps forward and then backward! He or she ends up in the same place he or she started! Since the volunteer split the number you gave him or her (2) in half, too, you subtract half of 2 (1) and end up with the number the volunteer rolled.

Example:

Roll a 6.	6
Six doubled is 12.	$6 + 6 = 12$
Add 2 which equals 14.	$12 + 2 = 14$
Divide that number in half which equals 7.	7
Subtract 1 and you are back at the number you rolled in the first place, 6.	$7 - 1 = 6$

You can also do this trick without using a die. Ask the volunteer to pick any number as high or as low as he or she wants. Since the magic depends on the number you choose, it will always work no matter what number the person picks, even if he or she picks one million.

I've Got Your Number: Doubling, Halving, Addition, Subtraction

Name _____ Date _____

Now you try it:

1. Roll a die. Write the number here.

2. Double the number you rolled.

3. Add 2 to the answer.

4. Divide that number in half.

5. Subtract 1 and end up with the number you rolled in the first place. TA-DA!

Remember, when you double a number and then divide it in half, you end up with the number you began with. In this trick, you added a 2 to the number that was rolled. When the answer was divided in half, the 2 you added was split in half along with the number you rolled on the die. Half of 2 is 1. If you add a different number, just subtract half of that number and you will have the correct answer. Pretty tricky, don't you think?

How did you do?

Materials (What props did you use?)

Procedure (How did you do the trick?)

Conclusion (What makes the magic work?)

Equations (What equations did you use to make the trick work?)

Chapter IV
MONEY MADNESS
✳ ✳ ✳ ✳ ✳ ✳ ✳ ✳ ✳ ✳
Teacher Notes

The math computation and reasoning for all the tricks in this chapter is easy. For any of the tricks use other small objects if coins are not available.

Also, in order to give the audience a good view of what is happening in the tricks, using an overhead projector is recommended. You will probably want to use a piece of clear plastic over the glass of the projector to protect it from scratching.

Trick 23. Evening the Odds: Addition, Even and Odd Numbers**
An even number of coins will be turned into an odd number and an odd number of coins will be turned into an even number.

Trick 24. Leftovers, Anyone? Subtraction**
Without looking, the magician will be able to tell how many coins are left after some have been taken away.

Trick 25. Hidden Coins: Addition, Subtraction**
A volunteer moves coins in three separate steps and, without looking, the magician knows exactly how many coins the person is hiding.

Trick 26. Whatever You Say: Addition, Even and Odd Numbers**
The magician will be able to predict whether coins chosen secretly by a volunteer added to those held by the magician will come out even or odd when added together.

Trick 27. Penny Pick: Addition, Subtraction, Halving**
Without looking the magician will tell someone how many pennies he or she has.

✳ ✳ ✳ ✳ ✳ ✳ ✳ ✳ ✳ ✳ ✳

Teacher Script

You're going to learn some tricks using money but, even though these tricks call for using coins, they work just as well with buttons, stones, or checkers. We'll use whatever is handy.

In some of the tricks we may be using an overhead projector so that everyone can see what is happening with the coins. These tricks involve laying coins out on a table and it will be easier for the audience to know what is happening if they see what you're doing projected on a wall.

So, on to Money Madness!

Evening the Odds:
Addition, Even and Odd Numbers

Suggested introduction: **I can turn an odd number of coins into an even number or an even number of coins into an odd number!**

THE PROPS

20 or more coins

overhead projector

THE TRICK

1. Lay out the coins on the table or projector.
2. Pick up an *odd* number of coins and hold them in your hand. Choose a volunteer, then turn your back.
3. Say: **Now you take away as many coins as you want.**
4. Say: **If you have left an *odd* number of coins, I will turn them into an *even* number with the coins I picked. If you have left an *even* number of coins, I will turn them into an *odd* number.**
5. Ask the volunteer to count the coins left on the projector and tell whether the number of coins is even or odd.
6. Open your hand and add your coins to the coins on the projector. If the volunteer had left an *even* number of coins, the number will now be *odd*. If the volunteer had left an *odd* number, the number will now be *even*.

THE MAGIC

If you make sure you have an *odd* number of coins in your hand, you will always be able to change an *odd* number into an *even* number or an *even* number into an *odd* number.

Why does this work?

You are holding an *odd* number of coins in your hand. An *odd* number added to an *even* number always comes out *odd*. An *odd* number added to an *odd* number always comes out *even*.

Evening the Odds:
Addition, Even and Odd Numbers

Name _____ Date _____

Now you try it:

To change an even number to an odd number:

1. Hold an *odd* number of coins in your hand.

2. Lay out an *even* number of coins on a table or on your desk.

3. Add the coins from your hand to those you have laid out. The total number of coins will be *odd*.

To change an odd number to an even number:

1. Hold an *odd* number of coins in your hand.

2. Lay out an *odd* number of coins on a table or on your desk.

3. Add the coins from your hand to those you have laid out. The total number of coins will be *even*.

Remember: An *odd* number added to an *even* number always comes out *odd*.

An *odd* number added to an *odd* number always comes out *even*.

How did you do?

Materials (What props did you use?)

Procedure (How did you do the trick?)

Conclusion (What makes the magic work?)

Equations (What equations did you use to make the trick work?)

Leftovers, Anyone? Subtraction

Suggested introduction: **Without looking, I will tell you how many pennies are left on the table after you take some away.**

THE PROPS

any *even* number of coins above 20

overhead projector

THE TRICK

1. Give a volunteer an *even* number of pennies.
2. Turn your back or put on your blindfold.
3. Say: **Make two rows of pennies with the same number of pennies in each row.**
4. Say: **Now take one penny from the bottom row.**
5. Say: **Take as many pennies from the top row as you want. Tell me how many you took.**
   (IMPORTANT: Be sure to remember this number!)
6. Say: **Count how many pennies are left in the top row. Take that many pennies from the bottom row.**
7. Say: **Now take away all the pennies from the top row.**
8. The volunteer tells you how many pennies he or she took from the top row in step 5.
9. You subtract 1 from the number the volunteer gives you and that is how many pennies are left.
10. Say some magic words and then announce how many pennies are left.

THE MAGIC

Follow the directions exactly, step by step, and you will always know how many coins are left on the table.

Why does this work?

This trick works because, one step at a time, the volunteer takes all the pennies away except for the number he or she told you in step 5 minus the one penny he or she took away in the first step.

Figure 4.1 Steps in Performing Leftovers, Anyone?

Step 1: Make two rows of pennies with the same number in each row.

Step 2: Take one penny from the bottom row.

Step 3: Take as many pennies from the top row as you want (for example, three).

Step 4: Count how many are left in the top row and take that many from the bottom row.

Step 5: Take away all the pennies in the top row.

Result: You are left with two pennies, which is one less than the volunteer took away in step three.

Leftovers, Anyone? Subtraction

Name _____ Date _____

Now you try it:

1. Make two equal rows of pennies.
2. Take one penny from the bottom row.
3. Take as many as you want from the top row. *Remember this number. Write it down if you want to.*
4. Count how many pennies are left in the top row and take that many away from the bottom row.
5. Take all the pennies away from the top row.
6. How many are left? If you followed the instructions exactly, there should be one less than the number you wrote down. Aren't numbers great? They make magic tricks so easy to do!

How did you do?

Materials (What props did you use?)

Procedure (How did you do the trick?)

Conclusion (What makes the magic work?)

Equations (What equations did you use to make the trick work?)

Hidden Coins: Addition, Subtraction

Suggested introduction: **I will correctly guess how many coins are in someone's hand!**

THE PROPS

20 coins

overhead projector

THE TRICK

1. Lay out the 20 coins on the overhead projector.
2. Turn your back and ask a volunteer to take any number of coins from 1 to 9 and put them in an empty pocket.
3. Say: **Count how many coins are left and add the two digits of that number.** (For example, if 15 are left, he or she will add 1 and 5 to make 6.)
4. Say: **Take that number of coins and put them in your pocket, too.**
5. Say: **Now take any number of coins and hide them in your hand.**
6. Turn around, count how many coins are left on the projector, and subtract that number from 9.
7. Your answer is the number of coins in the volunteer's hand. If no coins are left, the volunteer is holding 9 coins. If 9 coins are left, the volunteer's hand is empty.

THE MAGIC

The number of coins in the person's pocket will always be 11 no matter how many coins are taken at first. Since 20 minus 11 equals 9, there will be 9 coins left until the person takes some to hold in his or her hand.

Why does this work?

You know there should be 9 coins left. If there are not 9, you subtract the number of coins left from 9. That will tell you how many coins are hidden in the volunteer's hand.

> **Example:**
>
> Lay out 20 coins on a table.
>
> Take any number of coins and put them in your pocket. Let's say you take 6 coins.
>
> Count the number of coins left (14) and add those two digits together (1 + 4 = 5).
>
> Take five coins and put them in your pocket, too.
>
> No matter how many coins you take in the first step, you will always end up with 11 in your pocket.
>
> You should have 11 coins in your pocket and 9 left on the table.
>
> You will always know how many coins are now taken because you know there should be 9 left.

Hidden Coins: Addition, Subtraction

Name _____ Date _____

Now you try it:

1. Ask a friend to practice this trick with you.

2. Lay out 20 coins on a table and put on your blindfold.

3. Ask your friend to take any number of coins from 1 to 9 and put them in a pocket.

4. Tell him or her to count the number of coins left and add together the two digits in that number.

5. Tell him or her to take that many coins and put them in the pocket, too. There should be 9 coins left on the table.

6. Tell him or her to take as many coins as he or she wants and hold them in his or her hand.

7. Open your eyes and tell them how many coins are in your friend's hand.

You know there should be 9 coins left. If there are not 9 left, subtract the number of coins on the table from 9 to find out how many coins your friend is hiding. If there are 9 coins left, then your friend did not take any coins. If there are no coins left, then your friend took 9 coins (all of them).

How did you do?

Materials (What props did you use?)

Procedure (How did you do the trick?)

Conclusion (What makes the magic work?)

Equations (What equations did you use to make the trick work?)

Whatever You Say: Addition, Even and Odd Numbers

Suggested introduction: **I will be able to tell you whether the coins you secretly pick added to the coins I have in my hand will come out even or odd.**

THE PROPS

20 coins–pennies, nickels, and dimes mixed and laid out on a table or projector

THE TRICK

1. You take some coins and hold them in your hand.
2. Ask someone to choose some coins and hold them in his or her hand.
3. Say: **I predict that when you add your coins to my coins, we will get an *even* number.**
4. Put your coins together. Add the *number* of coins you have to the volunteer's if it will come out *even*. Add the *value* of your coins if that will make it come out an *even* number.

For instance, if the volunteer picks three pennies and you pick a dime and a penny, add the value of the coins to get 14, an *even* number: 3 cents + 11 cents = 14 cents.

If the volunteer picks two pennies and you pick a dime and a penny, add the coins to get 4, an *even* number: 2 coins + 2 coins = 4 coins.

THE MAGIC

This trick is easy to do because you choose whatever count will make your prediction come true.

Why does this work?

You either add how much the coins are worth or how many coins you have to make the count come out the way you predicted. It's trickery!

Whatever You Say: Addition, Even and Odd Numbers

Name _____ Date _____

Now you try it:

1. Lay about 20 mixed coins out on a table.
2. Choose a few and hold them in your hand.
3. Ask someone to take a few and hold them.
4. Predict that when you add your coins together, you will get an *even* number.
5. Put your coins together.
6. Add either the value of the coins or the number of coins to get an *even* number. Your prediction will never be wrong.

How did you do?

Materials (What props did you use?)

Procedure (How did you do the trick?)

Conclusion (What makes the magic work?)

Equations (What equations did you use to make the trick work?)

Penny Pick: Addition, Subtraction, Halving

Suggested introduction: **I will be able to tell you how many pennies you have in your hand at the end of this trick.**

THE PROPS

30 pennies

THE TRICK

1. Put on your blindfold and ask someone to choose any number of pennies from 1 to 6.

2. Tell the volunteer to take that many again plus 1 extra penny.

3. Tell the volunteer to take 9 more pennies.

4. Ask the volunteer to put half of his or her pennies back in the pile.

5. Now ask the volunteer to put the number of pennies he or she took in the first place back in the pile.

6. Now you say some magic words and tell the volunteer he or she has 5 pennies left.

THE MAGIC

The volunteer adds and subtracts the number of pennies he or she took. That leaves the volunteer with only the number of pennies you tell him or her to take.

Why does this work?

The volunteer takes some pennies in the first step. Later on he or she puts that same number back into the pile. You tell the volunteer to take one more than he or she took in the first place. Then you tell him or her to take 9 pennies. Nine and 1 are 10. When the volunteer splits the number in half, he or she is left with 5 pennies because 5 is half of 10.

Penny Pick:
Addition, Subtraction, Halving

Name _____ Date _____

Now you try it:

1. Lay out 30 pennies.
2. Take any number of pennies from 1 to 6.
3. Take that number again plus 1 extra.
4. Take 9 more pennies.
5. Now put half of your pennies back.
6. Put the number of pennies you took in the first place back. Do you have 5 pennies left? Of course you do. You're a magician!

How did you do?

Materials (What props did you use?)

Procedure (How did you do the trick?)

Conclusion (What makes the magic work?)

Equations (What equations did you use to make the trick work?)

Chapter V
MEASURING MALARKEY
✳ ✳ ✳ ✳ ✳ ✳ ✳ ✳ ✳ ✳ ✳

Teacher Notes

Here are some tricks that involve measuring. A tape measure should be used in the first trick which is especially easy to do.

Trick 28. Funny Feet: Measuring**
The magician will be able to tell a volunteer how long his or her foot is without measuring it.

Trick 29. Lucky Lengths: Measuring, Addition, Subtraction
Without knowing what a measured object is, the magician will be able to tell its length.

Trick 30. Double Magic: Measuring, Addition, Subtraction with Borrowing, Doubling
Without knowing what two measured objects are, the magician will be able to tell the lengths of both.

✳ ✳ ✳ ✳ ✳ ✳ ✳ ✳ ✳ ✳ ✳

Teacher Script

Now we are going to do some tricks that involve measuring. You will be able to magically tell how long someone's foot is, and also correctly tell how long objects are that someone has measured.

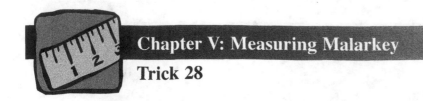

Funny Feet: Measuring

Suggested introduction: **I am going to tell you how long your foot is without ever measuring it.**

THE PROPS

tape measure

pad and pencil

THE TRICK

1. Ask for a volunteer and ask him or her if you may measure his or her arm, around his or her head, and his or her hand.

2. Using a tape measure, measure the person's arm from shoulder to elbow, lower arm from elbow to wrist, around his or her head, and his or her hand from the wrist to the tip of the middle finger. Write down and label your measurements, but do not let anyone see your numbers.

3. Say: **I have not measured your foot, but because of my magic powers, I know exactly how long your foot is.**

4. Say some magic words and tell the volunteer the measurement of his or her foot. It will be the same as the distance you measured from the elbow to the wrist.

5. Ask the volunteer to take off his or her shoe and measure his or her foot. It will be just as long as you said!

THE MAGIC

The length of a person's foot is the same as the distance from the wrist to the elbow.

All you have to do to make this trick work is to make sure you measure correctly and label the numbers as you write them down. You take several measurements to trick the audience.

Example:

Shoulder to elbow: 10 inches

Elbow to wrist: 8 inches

Around head: 15 inches

Hand: 5 inches

The person's foot will be 8 inches long.

Funny Feet: Measuring

Name _____ Date _____

Now you try it:

Use a tape measure. Write down the numbers as you measure.

Measure:

      from your shoulder to your elbow,   _____

      from your elbow to your wrist,   _____

      around your head,   _____

      and from your wrist to the tip of your middle finger. _____

Your foot should be the same length as the distance between your elbow and your wrist.

Measure from your elbow to your wrist and write that measurement here. _____

Measure your foot and write that measurement here. _____

Do the numbers match? They should.

How did you do?

Materials (What props did you use?)

Procedure (How did you do the trick?)

Conclusion (What makes the magic work?)

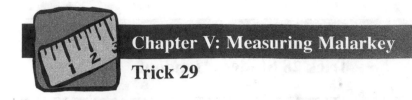

Lucky Lengths:
Measuring, Addition, Subtraction

Suggested introduction: **I will be able to tell you the size of the object you measure.**

THE PROPS

dark-colored marker

large piece of paper

six-inch or twelve-inch ruler

THE TRICK

1. Give a volunteer the ruler and marker and put on your blindfold.
2. Say: **Measure something in the room. Round the number to the closest inch and write that number on the paper. Let me know when you are done.**
3. Say: **Pretend that the object you measured is 10 times bigger that it really is. Add a zero behind your number. That makes it ten times bigger.**
4. Say: **There are 12 inches in a foot. Add 12 to the number.**
5. Say: **There are 36 inches in a yard. Add 36 to the number.**
6. Say: **Tell me your final answer and I will tell you how long the object is.**
7. In your head you cross out the last number. Subtract 4 from the number that is left and you will have the length of the object the volunteer measured. Say some magic words and tell him or her the answer.

   Example:

The volunteer measures something that is 7 inches long.	7
He or she makes it ten times bigger by adding a zero.	70
He or she adds 12 inches.	82
He or she adds 36 inches.	118
You cross off the last number.	11
Subtract 4.	$11 - 4 = 7$

   You are left with 7, the length of the object that was measured.

THE MAGIC

This trick works every time if you remember to cross out the number that is in the ones column.

Why does this work?

The volunteer adds 12 and 36 to the number. That makes four 10's and eight 1's. We cross out the ones place. We just care about the four 10's. We subtract 4 from the final answer and that gives us the length of the object that was measured.

Lucky Lengths:
Measuring, Addition, Subtraction

Name _____ Date _____

Now you try it:

1. Measure an object, round it off to the nearest inch, and write the number down.

2. Pretend it is ten times bigger than it really is. Place a zero after the number.

3. There are 12 inches in a foot. Add 12.

4. There are 36 inches in a yard. Add 36.

5. Cross off the number in the ones column.

6. Subtract 4.

7. Do you have the length of the object you measured? You should have. After all, you are a magician!

How did you do?

Materials (What props did you use?)

Procedure (How did you do the trick?)

Conclusion (What makes the magic work?)

Equations (What equations did you use to make the magic work?)

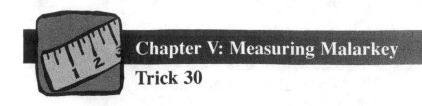

Double Magic: Measuring, Addition, Subtraction with Borrowing, Doubling

Suggested introduction: **I will be able to tell you the lengths of two objects that you measure.**

THE PROPS
dark-colored marker
piece of paper
six-inch or twelve-inch ruler

THE TRICK

1. Give someone the ruler and the marker and put your blindfold on.
2. Say: **Measure two objects in the room and write down how long they are on the paper. Tell me when you are done.**
3. Say: **Choose one of the numbers and add it five times.**
4. Say: **Add 6. Then double your answer.**
5. Say: **Add the length of the second object.**
6. Say: **Tell me the answer and I will tell you the length of both objects.**
7. In your mind subtract 12 from the answer and say the two numbers that are left. They will be the length of the two things that were measured.

Example:

Two objects measured.	7 and 9
Pick one and add it five times.	$7 + 7 + 7 + 7 + 7 = 35$
Add 6.	$35 + 6 = 41$
Double the answer.	$41 + 41 = 82$
Add the length of the second object.	$82 + 9 = 91$
Subtract 12.	$91 - 12 = 79$

You end up with the lengths of the two objects that were measured.

THE MAGIC
You trick the volunteer into giving you the lengths of the two things he or she measured.

Why does this work?
When the volunteer adds one of the numbers five times and then doubles it, it is just like adding a zero to the original number. The volunteer picks 7, adds it five times and doubles it to 70. When he or she adds the second number to 70, he or she gets 79. Those are the volunteer's two measurements. The volunteer does not know he or she is telling you his or her numbers because you told him or her to add a 6. The 6 gets doubled to 12. Only you know that you can get the volunteer's numbers by subtracting 12.

Double Magic: Measuring, Addition, Subtraction with Borrowing, Doubling

Name _____ Date _____

Now you try it:

1. Measure two objects and write the numbers down.

2. Pick one of the numbers and add it five times.

3. Add 6.

4. Double the answer.

5. Add the other measurement.

6. Subtract 12.

7. You should have the two numbers you started with. That's magic!

How did you do?

Materials (What props did you use?)

Procedure (How did you do the trick?)

Conclusion (What makes the magic work?)

Equations (What equations did you use to make the magic work?)

Linworth Learning